Introdu

Machynlleth's magnifice between the Pumlumons access to the coast, make in the midst of some of Wales' fines passes both the north and south side as the seaside resorts of Aberdyfi and Borth, and inland to Dylife and Cemmaes. It provides an excellent introduction to the UNESCO *Dyfi Biosphere Area* – a very special place for people and nature – and the only such area in Wales.

All of the routes can be undertaken by a reasonably fit person, with **Walk 17** being the most demanding. Walking boots or stout shoes are recommended for all the walks, and a waterproof anorak is a sensible idea if the weather is changeable. A weather forecast (charge) can be obtained by calling 09068 500414, or visit www. weathercall.co.uk. *And remember always* that this is sheep farming country – if you wish to be accompanied by your dog, *you must keep it on a lead at all times.*

The location of each walk is shown on the back cover, and a summary of the key characteristics of each is also given. All of the routes follow public rights of way, permissive paths or Forestry Commission tracks, and have been checked. Things do change how-ever, so don't always assume you have lost your way if what you find differs from the information in this book. Instructions to reach the start of each walk are given from the Clock Tower in Machynlleth. A very useful *unofficial* Information Centre is run in a gift shop at the Glyndŵr Centre in Maengwyn Street, Machynlleth. There are also useful *Tourist Information Centres* in *Aberdyfi* and *Borth*, both open in season.

This new expanded edition provides five more excellent walks, taking you to the Afon Dyfi, Parc Common, the Centre for Alternative Technology, Cemmaes and the *exciting* New Darowen Panorama.

Please always respect local traditions, and care for the environ-ment, so that all those who want to share the great charm and beauty of this special area may continue to do so.

Enjoy your walking!

AN ABERDYFI PANORAMA

DESCRIPTION This gentle hilly 3½-mile walk soon gets you up above Aberdyfi, enjoying fine views over the mouth of the Dyfi estuary and south towards Borth and Aberystwyth. The descent is through a very pretty cwm (valley), followed by a path through the dunes, or by the shore (option 2). Allow 2 hours.
START The Tourist Information Centre, Aberdyfi. SN 614959.

DIRECTIONS From the Clock Tower in Machynlleth, take the A487 north to cross the Dyfi Bridge and turn left onto the A493. Continue to Aberdyfi, where there is a large car park on the left, just beyond the Tourist Information Centre. Or you can take the excellent train journey from Machynlleth to Aberdyfi.

1 From the Tourist Information Centre walk to the RIGHT, then take the first LEFT into Copperhill Street. Continue up the street, passing under the railway bridge.

3 Cross this road, and go through the wooden gate opposite. Turn LEFT, following the direction indicated by the arrow. *As you climb, superb coastal views open up.* The path follows the edge of the field, climbing gently, then quite steeply, to reach a stile.

2 After the fifth house beyond the railway bridge, take the path to the LEFT, which climbs uphill, and is joined by a path from the right just after No 2 Bryniau-Isaf. Turn sharp RIGHT here and climb steeply up this path. Continue ahead when the path widens and becomes a tarmac road. Continue along the road, passing between houses to join another road.

A493 to Tywyn
6
Cwm Safn-ast
Trefeddian-fach 5
Golf Course
Dunes
Old Coastguard Station
Trefeddian Farm
Trefeddian Hotel
Yr Horc
4
Dunes
A493
Station
Afon Dyfi

4 Cross the stile, and continue with a fence to your left. Cross another stile in the corner of the field, and carry on ahead, to eventually descend to the footpath arrow to the right-hand side of *Trefeddian Farm*. Cross the small stream by the sign, go through the gate and turn LEFT following the direction indicated to walk around the back of the farm buildings. Go through the waymarked gateway, then turn RIGHT passing caravans. After about 15 yards, look down to locate a small footbridge over a stream, with a stile just beyond. Descend to the stream and cross them both.

5 From the stile, walk ahead, uphill, for about 10 yards to reach a small brow, then walk half-LEFT across the field, with a low summit to the right. Soon the handsome, but derelict, stone buildings of *Trefeddian-fach* come into view. Walk past these and continue ahead, following the path between low summits. The path joins a track. Turn LEFT to reach a tarmac lane, which you follow down through Cwm Safn-ast.

6 Now pass through a gate, opposite the cemetery, turn LEFT and go through a gate to reach the coast road. Cross the road, veering slightly RIGHT, to go down waymarked track to the railway. Pass through the gates and *CAREFULLY* cross the railway, looking and listening for trains. Continue ahead along the track. *You are now crossing Aberdyfi Golf Course, so watch out for fast moving golf balls.* Continue to cross a wooden walkway to the beach. Turn LEFT to return to Aberdyfi along the sands.

*A*berdyfi *is a pretty resort village in an enviable situation, facing south across the Dyfi estuary and sheltered by steep hills to the north. It is well known for the folk song 'The Bells of Aberdovey', composed around 1785 by Charles Dibdin, and featured in his Drury Lane musical 'Liberty Hall'. The bells now lie under the sea with Cantre'r Gwaelod, the Lowland Hundred, which was at one time a low fertile plain protected by sea walls, supporting several villages and towns. In legend the sea walls were in the care of Prince Seithennin, a warrior of Lord Gwyddno Garanhir, and this was unfortunate, as Seithennin's main preoccupation was with feasting and drinking, rendering him drunk most of the time. Eventually, during the sixth century, the inevitable southwesterly gale coincided with a high tide. Seithennin had let maintenance slip and the walls were breached: the land disappeared beneath the waves, never to be reclaimed. It may well have been that all the activity in the region did take place to the west of Aberdyfi, since in 1569 it was recorded that there were only three dwellings in here, even though herring fleets often sought shelter in the estuary.*

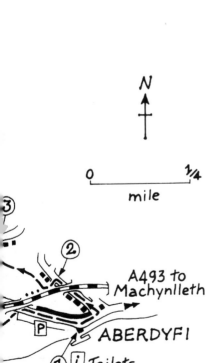

N

0 — ¼ mile

A493 to Machynlleth

ABERDYFI

P

Toilets

START

WALK 2
ABOVE PICNIC ISLAND

DESCRIPTION The effort involved in the initial climb on this 4-mile walk is repaid many times over by stunning views (on a clear day) over the Dyfi estuary and the whole sweep of Cardigan Bay, from Bardsey in the north to Strumble Head, Pembrokeshire, in the south. The last ¼ mile, given suitable tides, includes the Roman Road. Allow 2½ hours.
START The lay-by at Picnic Island, on the A493 between Machynlleth and Aberdyfi. SN 626963.

DIRECTIONS From the Clock Tower in Machynlleth, take the A487 north to cross the Dyfi Bridge and turn left onto the A493 towards Aberdyfi. After about 9½ miles look out for the clearly signposted 'Outward Bound Wales' on the right. Park in the next lay-by on the left, at the entrance to Picnic Island. Or you can take the train from Machynlleth to Penhelig Station and start the walk from there. You could also use the car park in Aberdyfi.

1 From Picnic Island, walk to the RIGHT along the road for about 100 yards to reach a footpath sign on the north side of the road, just before the entrance to the Outward Bound. Following the direction indicated by the sign, cross the stone wall, turn LEFT and walk up the path beside a stream. Cross the footbridge, turn RIGHT to climb steps and continue. Soon you join a tarmac road by the Outward Bound rope course. Now walk along the rear of the buildings and then head slightly left gently uphill on a path, going through a metal gate and then passing an old corrugated iron garage building, to reach a footpath sign ahead, by a track which crosses your route.

2 DO NOT follow the direction (right) indicated by the sign, but continue ahead, walking gently uphill on a pleasant grassy field. *Pause at the first summit to look back over the estuary, and enjoy the first of many fine views on this walk.* When the track veers left DO NOT follow it, but continue ahead, starting to descend towards trees. A path appears, and soon you arrive at a well hidden footpath sign. Continue in the direction indicated, going through a gate. Gradually the path descends more steeply (take care!) to a gate in the corner.

3 Go through and turn left to walk along a tarmac lane, crossing a cattle grid and continuing up the lane to *Trefrifawr, an extremely handsome vernacular farmhouse, dating from the 17th-18thC.* Enter the yard, walk to the right of the house and turn LEFT,

following the direction indicated on the footpath sign, to reach a gate.

4 Go through the gate and continue along the path uphill, with a stream down to your right. Eventually you come to a ladder stile. Cross it and follow the track, which veers to the right. Cross a farm track and continue ahead, to reach a tarmac lane.

5 Turn LEFT to walk along the lane, passing through a gate on your way. *On a clear day the Llyn Peninsula can be seen stretching along the horizon to Bardsey Island. Soon the view encompasses the whole of Cardigan Bay, as far south as Strumble Head.* Eventually the lane begins to descend, and a lane joins from the left.

6 Turn left into this lane, signed for the Wales Coastal Path (WCP), and walk downhill. Go through a gate and continue for about 60 yards to a waymarked gate on the right. Go through the gate and walk half-LEFT down the hill, looking for a waymark post ahead. Locate the post and walk in the direction indicated, to a gap in a hedge with another waymark post. Go through the gap, turn right and walk to the next post. Cross the stile below it, cross the bridge over the stream and walk downhill, beside the stream, to a stile.

7 Cross the stile and then walk down to a gate, and go through. Follow the path, which climbs gently. When you reach a gate, go through and continue along the path.

Soon the path starts to descend. Follow the path, going through a gate and eventually, passing stables on the left. Cross the stile ahead and continue along a path now sheltered by a tangle of blackberry and broom and passing a WCP waymark to reach a gate.

8 Go through this and follow the path downhill, going through a gate. The path finally descends steps beside houses to join a lane. Turn right, then immediately left, to continue the descent. When you reach the main road, turn left.

9 Just before the railway crosses over the road, opposite the Penhelig Hotel, turn RIGHT to walk by the river. When you rejoin the main road, you have a choice of routes to return to Picnic Island.

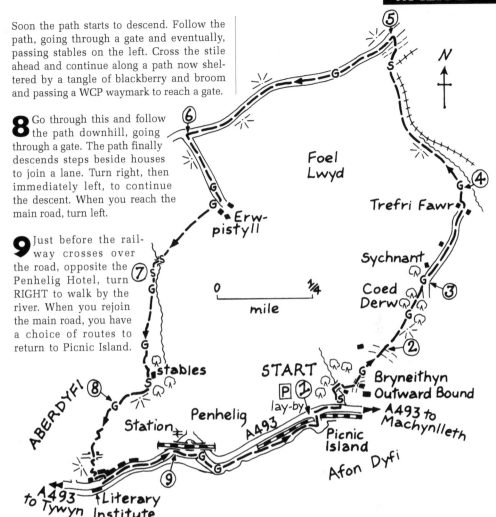

If the tides are favourable – either low or falling – you can turn immediately right to go through a metal gate, and then a kissing gate, to follow the old Roman Road back to Picnic Island. **But do take care**, as at certain states of the tide parts of this path can be covered; it can also be slippery when wet; and young children need to be carefully watched if the tide is high. **If you are at all unsure**, then return to the start of the walk along the road. If you have walked along the Roman Road, climb the steps at Picnic Island, cross the bridge over the railway, and return to your car.

*T*he railway between Dovey Junction and Aberdyfi was constructed in 1867 at great expense, as the residents of Aberdyfi insisted it passed through the village in two tunnels, to remain hidden. The spoil from these tunnels was dumped by the foreshore at Penhelig, and Penhelig Terrace was subsequently built on top. The station here was an afterthought, being built in 1933.

WALK 3
LLYN BARFOG THE BEARDED LAKE

DESCRIPTION A short and popular 2½ mile walk from Happy Valley which soon gets you up in the hills enjoying the charms of this lake, with its legendary associations. This is followed by exciting views over the Dyfi estuary on your return. Allow 2 hours.

START From the Snowdonia National Park car park in Happy Valley. SN 641986.

DIRECTIONS From the Clock Tower in Machynlleth, take the A487 north to cross the Dyfi Bridge and turn left onto the A493. When you reach Cwrt, about 5 miles from Machynlleth, fork right onto the road signposted 'Cwm Maethlon – Happy Valley'. After 3½ miles turn left into the car park for the Bearded Lake (look out for the sign, it is easily missed from this direction!).

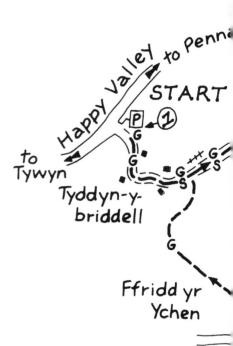

1 Leave the car park by the gate in the far right-hand corner, turn LEFT and walk along the track, which curves past farm buildings. When you reach a gate, go through and continue ahead. Cross another gate and ladder-stile and follow the track. The track passes a ford to the left, then bends left in front of a house to reach a gate with a very tall ladder stile beside it. Cross this and continue.

2 When the track bears to the left, follow the direction indicated by the sign along a grassy path which passes a scruffy mast. This path soon rejoins the track. Continue ahead to pass through the next gate and ladder-stile *noting the fine view to the west.* The track climbs uphill, then curves to the left – but you continue ahead to another gate and ladder-stile, which you cross to reach Llyn Barfog, the Bearded Lake. Go through a small gate to gain easy access to the water's edge. *There is a fine view from the cairn on the eastern side. The lake is in a beautifully isolated situation, its surface covered in water-lilies from late June until September. This*

may have given it its name, although those more romantically inclined would rather it were named in honour of one of King Arthur's knights – in particular 'the bearded one'. Barfog may have even been Arthur's foster father. There is also, not surprisingly, a fairy-tale associated with the lake, concerning a magical cow which came into the possession of a farmer of Dysyrnant, half-a-mile to the north. This beast gave birth to many fine calves, and provided many gallons of creamy milk. The farmer, as a consequence, became rich. But eventually the cow grew too old, and the farmer decided to employ a butcher to slaughter her. But as the butcher was about to kill the cow, the knife fell from his hand. A little green fairy woman appeared from by the lake, and called the cow, and her calves, home. The fairy and the cows then disappeared into the lake. From then on the farmer's luck changed for the worse. Continue a little way further to reach a stone that directs you to an 'echo'. Walk a little way to a summit overlooking a valley and try a shout!

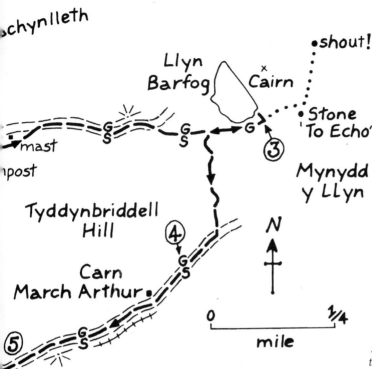

chynlleth

Llyn Barfog

Cairn

•shout!

•Stone 'To Echo'

Mynydd y Llyn

mast

post

Tyddynbriddell Hill

④

③

N

Carn March Arthur

⑤

0   ¼
mile

with the alignment. Another tale says it was left by Arthur's horse after he had dragged a monster from Llyn Barfog. Or maybe it was left by Huw Gadarn, otherwise known as 'Huw the Mighty', who captured a monster and dragged it into the lake. You can take your pick. Huw Gadarn is thought to have originated from Defrobane, which is now Istanbul, about 1800BC. He is said to have mnemonically systematised the learnings of Druids, who he led west. He claimed great intellectual powers, and is also reputed to be responsible for the founding of Stonehenge, the introduction of glass-making and Ogham script. He established that the 'Gorsedd', or assembly of Druids and Bards, should be held in an open grassy space, in full view of the people. Continue along the track, crossing the next gate and stile. Soon the track starts to descend.

3 After enjoying your stay at the lake, retrace your steps through the small gate and, about 100 yards from the edge of the lake, turn LEFT along a green path between two low summits. Continue along the green path, eventually veering RIGHT to join a track, *which is part of the Panorama Walk.*

4 You come to a gate and ladder-stile. Cross them and continue ahead. *Soon stunning views over the Dyfi estuary open up to the south. A slate slab on the right marks 'Carn March Arthur'. Here you will see an indentation in the rock, in legend said to be the hoof-print of Arthur's horse. One tale says it was left when Arthur and his horse leapt across the Dyfi when pursued by his enemies, but the observant (and cynical) will not be satisfied*

5 You reach two gates by a house. Take the RIGHT-hand gate, following the direction indicated by the National Park sign. Continue downhill, passing through a gate and bearing slightly RIGHT to rejoin your outward route by the very tall ladder stile. Cross this to return to the car park.

CARN MARCH ARTHUR

WALK 4
DOWN BY THE DYFI

DESCRIPTION The initial part of this 3-mile walk traverses the flood plain of the River Dyfi, the haunt of wildfowl and duck. A short section beside the river leads to the return through woods and over gentle hills. Try to make time for a visit to the church in Pennal. Allow 2 hours.
START Behind the church at Pennal. SH 699004.
DIRECTIONS From the Clock Tower in Machynlleth, take the A487 north to cross the Dyfi Bridge and turn left onto the A493 towards Aberdyfi. After 3 miles you reach Pennal. Park behind the church.

I Walk to the main road by the church, and turn RIGHT. Cross the bridge, cross the road and walk along to a gate, with a footpath sign, on your LEFT. Go through the gate, and walk with a stream on your LEFT. Go through the next gate and veer to the RIGHT along a track, ignoring the ford.

2 Cross a wide concrete bridge and turn RIGHT to go through a gate. Turn LEFT and walk across the field to a drainage ditch. Walk with this ditch on your RIGHT. Cross a ditch to reach a gate and ladder stile. Go through and continue ahead.

3 When you reach a footbridge on your right, cross it and turn LEFT, crossing a ditch. After about 20 yards look for a ditch to your RIGHT. Walk beside this ditch. Eventually you climb a small embankment to reach the River Dyfi. *This is Llyn Draenog pool, where craft making their way up river to Derwenlas could ride out low water.* Turn RIGHT, to walk on the embankment with the river on your LEFT.

4 After a few yards you cross a stile, and then continue along the embankment. Ignore a stile down to your right, and continue until you reach a footbridge on your RIGHT. *A short distance to the south-east is the railway bridge over the Dyfi. This was officially opened on 14 August 1867. The first engine to cross the river under its own power was the Oswestry & Newtown's Volunteer, which had been transported from Ynyslas to Aberdyfi by barge, to return over the bridge on 30 July 1866, driven by John Ward. When built, the bridge had a 35 ft-wide opening section, which was drawn back under the superstructure to allow the passage of boats. It was finally permanently fixed in 1914. Dovey Junction Station, a lonely outpost, presented an entirely bleak prospect when first opened, with no shelter at all on the solitary platform.* Cross the footbridge and walk with a drainage ditch to your LEFT.

5 Go through the first gate on your LEFT, crossing the ditch, and turn RIGHT, *passing a lime kiln cut from the natural rock over to the left.* Go through the gate ahead and turn LEFT, then after a short distance turn RIGHT through a gate to join a tarmac lane, and follow this uphill and away from the farm buildings. Continue along the lane.

6 Pass a gate and an unofficial stile on the right to reach a waymarked gate on your right. Turn RIGHT here, go through the gate and continue along the track. Go through another gate and then veer left off the track to pass Penmaendovey on your left. Walk towards a waymarked telegraph pole, and continue ahead to a gate and stile.

7 Cross the stile and follow the path with a fence to your right, to come to a gate and stile. Cross the stile and follow the path with a fence to the right, and trees to the left. Cross the next stile and continue with a fence to the right to another stile, *enjoying an excellent view over the estuary.* Cross this and follow the path ahead gently downhill through trees, *thick with bluebells in the Spring.* When the path joins a track, turn LEFT and continue downhill, eventually crossing a temporary barrier.

8 As you reach the holiday bungalows at Plas Talgarth continue straight ahead, to eventually join the road out of the holiday park. Turn LEFT and walk along the access

8

road to reach the main road. *To the right of the access road, as you approach the main road, is* Tomen Las, *a prominent tree covered mound. It was from here that Owain Glyndŵr is said to have sent the 'Pennal Letter' in 1406, at a time when Europe had two Popes, one in Rome and one in Avignon in France. Glyndŵr's letter stated that the Welsh would support Benedict XIII, the French Pope, following certain conditions. Join the main road and turn RIGHT to return to Pennal.*

***T**ry to make time to visit the church of St Peter ad Vincula, one of only five such churches in Britain with that dedication. A church was founded on this site in the 6thC by St Tannwg and St Eithrias, Celtic missionaries who came from Brittany, although its oval churchyard*

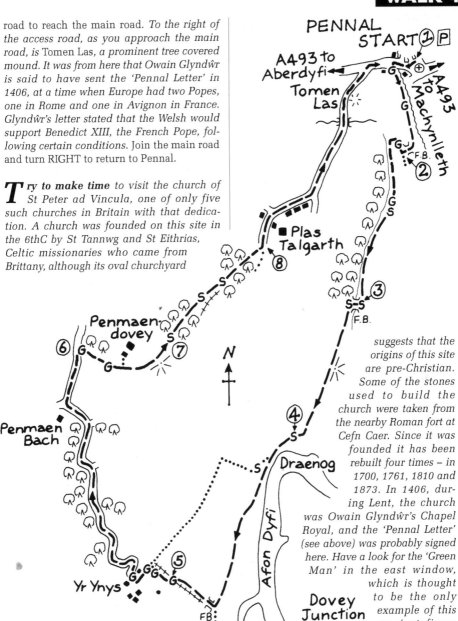

suggests that the origins of this site are pre-Christian. Some of the stones used to build the church were taken from the nearby Roman fort at Cefn Caer. Since it was founded it has been rebuilt four times – in 1700, 1761, 1810 and 1873. In 1406, during Lent, the church was Owain Glyndŵr's Chapel Royal, and the 'Pennal Letter' (see above) was probably signed here. Have a look for the 'Green Man' in the east window, which is thought to be the only example of this ancient figure in any church or chapel in Wales.

WOODLAND WANDERS ABOVE PENNAL

DESCRIPTION A 7-mile walk amidst the woodlands in the hills behind Pennal. Narrow valleys, ancient green tracks and the occasional sweeping view combine to make this a memorable walk. *A ford on this route can become impassable during wet weather, so please bear this in mind.* Allow 4 hours.

START Behind the church at Pennal. SH 699004.

DIRECTIONS From the Clock Tower in Machynlleth, take the A487 north to cross the Dyfi Bridge and turn left onto the A493 towards Aberdyfi. After 3 miles you reach Pennal. Park behind the church.

1 From the church, walk away from the main road, turn RIGHT at the junction and walk through Felindre and continue gently uphill. When the road forks (by a seat), head to the RIGHT and continue. Bear LEFT at the next fork (signed 'Cycleway 8') and continue, crossing the bridge over the Afon Pennal. Eventually you will reach *Ffarm Gyllellog.*

2 Go through the gate, cross the farmyard, go through a second gate and continue to a third gate. Go through, and enter the forest. Continue along the track to a junction. Remember this junction, as you will turn here on the return route.

3 Walk to the RIGHT, along the forestry road, which then gently curves to the left, with a stream down on the right.

4 At a footpath sign, just beyond a house away across the valley, veer half-RIGHT downhill towards the stream, where you cross a bridge and turn LEFT. Soon you join a forest road, where

you turn LEFT. After 40 yards fork half-RIGHT up a fine mossy green path through the trees. A path joins from the right, but continue ahead. The path climbs quite steeply. Eventually you emerge at a 'T' junction of forest roads.

5 Turn LEFT along the forest road and continue until the road makes a wide hairpin left. Here you will see a waymarked grassy track AHEAD. Follow this into the forest. The track soon traverses a muddy patch where a stream crosses. Veer LEFT here. The path begins to descend and soon joins a forest road, where you head to the RIGHT.

6 At the next junction (by forestry sign 'RO905') continue to the RIGHT for a few yards. Opposite a vehicle 'No Entry' sign turn sharp LEFT up a grassy track to a gate. Go through and head to the right up the field to a waymark post, which directs you to the right, with a Leylandii hedge on your left. You join a track, where you turn LEFT to pass between the buildings of *Maesywerngoch*, and through two gates (enclosing a flock of friendly geese!). Continue along the path, *which is now in part of a handsome informal garden containing over 20 types of camellia, and many rhododendrons.*

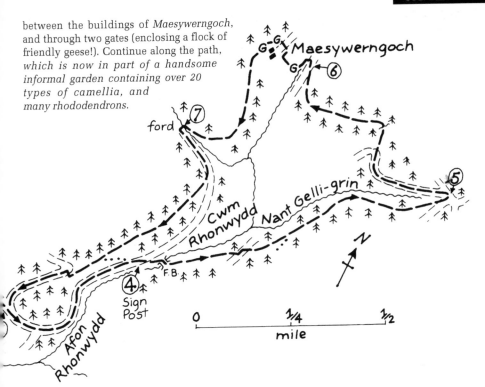

7 The path eventually descends to a ford, which you cross if safe to do so (**this can become impassable in wet weather**). Turn LEFT and walk along the forestry road for about 100 yards until you see a signed footpath heading into the trees on the RIGHT. Follow this path, *although tree felling operations may require a minor diversion here. If so, just stay on the forestry road until you reach a footpath signpost (which you passed on the outward route), where you fork right* up a track into the trees to rejoin the path. Continue along the track until you reach a felled area, just beyond a point where power lines cross overhead. Turn sharp RIGHT and walk 35 yards uphill to reach a forestry road. Turn LEFT here and continue along the road, which curves to the left. Look out for the junction with the track you came along at point **3**. Turn RIGHT here to walk back through the farmyard and along the road to Pennal.

11

WALK 6
BEACH & BOG AT BORTH

DESCRIPTION This full walk covers 5½ miles of a level route which encompasses the edge of Borth Bog and a fine stroll back along the sea front. It is easily reduced to a little over 3½ miles by making a shorter return walk. Whichever option you choose, you will find this an easy level route with extensive views of the surrounding hills and, on a clear day, the full sweep of Cardigan Bay. Allow 3 hours for the full walk, and take great care at all the railway level crossings.
START The car park on the golf course at Ynyslas or roadside at the northern end of Borth for the shorter walk . SN 606925.

DIRECTIONS From the Clock Tower in Machynlleth, take the A487 south towards Aberystwyth. After about 8½ miles, at Tre'r-ddol, turn right onto the B4353 and follow this until you join the coast road at a 'T' junction. Opposite is the entrance to a car park (modest charge in season). Drive in and park. You can also drive towards Borth and start your walk there – park at the roadside, near the station. You can take the train from Machynlleth to Borth, and begin your walk between instruction points 6 & 7.

1 *These are directions for the full walk.* From the car park, walk with the sea to your left, and look out for an old red-brick look-out post. *Ynyslas dunes were used as*

2 Walk along the track directly opposite, go through a gateway and continue ahead. Go through another three gates to emerge

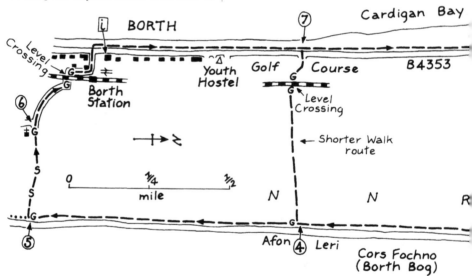

an artillery testing range during World War II. The great gun known as 'Big Bertha' was brought down from Scotland for testing here. Just before this there is a track to the right. Turn RIGHT along this track and *carefully* cross the golf course. Go through a gateway and cross the road.

on a tarmac track, where a lane joins from the right. Continue ahead towards the boat-yard. Cross a cattle grid and join the road. Continue ahead over the bridge, and continue to cross the level crossing **with great care, ensuring no trains are coming**.

3 Turn RIGHT through a gate and walk with the railway to your right. Continue ahead to cross the footbridge beside the railway bridge. Once off the bridge, turn left and cross the stile to continue with the river now on your left. *You are now walking by the River Leri and the Leri Fields where you can watch for Curlew, Snipe, Redshank, Black-Tailed Godwit and Whimbrel. The hide is back from the estuary itself towards the village of Borth and you have to use the public footpath across the golf course to get to it. Saltmarshes have formed where the River Leri runs into the Dyfi. On the other side of the Afon Leri is Cors Fochno (Borth Bog), renowned for its wild flowers, moths and adder population. Otters have been seen. Cors Fochno is a raised peat mire and has been designated a UNESCO biosphere reserve as one of the most impressive lowland raised bogs in the UK.*

4 You come to a gate where a track joins from the right. Go through the gate and continue with the river still to your left. *(If you are taking the shorter route, look out for the signposted footpath on the right which crosses the golf course and the railway through two gates – take great care, to reach point 7, where you turn RIGHT to return to the start.)*

5 You reach another gate: go through, leaving the nature reserve, and immediately turn RIGHT, walking with a small hill to your left. Continue ahead, crossing the next two stiles (keeping a rough hedge to your left). *This is the 'Uppingham Path', and you will notice two inscribed slate seats on the left, recording Uppingham School and the years 1876 and 1877. Borth's reputation as a health-giving resort had spread across England, and its restorative qualities were noted by the Reverend Thring of Uppingham in Rutland, whose village was suffering an epidemic. He evacuated the entire school to Borth, where they built a friendly and lasting relationship with the village. As well as the seats, the boys left a stained glass window and a lectern in the church.* Finally you go through a gate to join the lane below St Matthew's Church.

6 Turn RIGHT along the lane. At the level crossing **ensure that no trains are coming. If you can hear a train, WAIT until it has passed. If you have young children with you, make sure they are under control, and make sure they stay with you.** Go through the gate, cross the track, go through the opposite gate and turn RIGHT. Turn LEFT by the station to emerge at the seafront. Turn RIGHT.

7 Now walk along the beach, sea wall or road, with the sea to your left. *Before the last ice age, the coastline was over 7 miles further to the west. If you explore the beach at low water during Spring tides, you can see stumps of oak, pine, birch, willow and hazel (preserved by the acid anaerobic conditions in the peat), associated with the legend of Cantre'r Gwaelod.* Continue ahead to return to the car park

A STROLL ABOVE TRE'R-DDOL

DESCRIPTION A delightful 4-mile walk from the Wildfowler pub, on quiet farm roads which initially climb through woodlands to give expansive views across the Dyfi towards Aberdyfi. The road then passes along a quiet valley towards the old Bryndyfi mine, before descending back to Tre'r-ddol through farms and forestry. Allow 2½ hours.

START The Wildfowler pub in Tre'r-ddol. SN 659923.

DIRECTIONS From the Clock Tower in Machynlleth, take the A487 south towards Aberystwyth. After about 8½ miles, fork left into Tre'r-ddol and park at the roadside by the Wildfowler pub.

1 From the pub, walk towards the church, turning LEFT up the lane before the bridge. Continue along this lane, which climbs steeply uphill through woodland, and turns sharply right to pass through a gateway by *Llety-lwydin*. When the road reaches a T junction, turn LEFT.

2 Go through a gateway and continue. *When the road makes a very sharp left turn, you can continue ahead along the unsurfaced lane. Through the second gate on the right a track leads to the extensive remains of the Bryndyfi Lead Mine.*

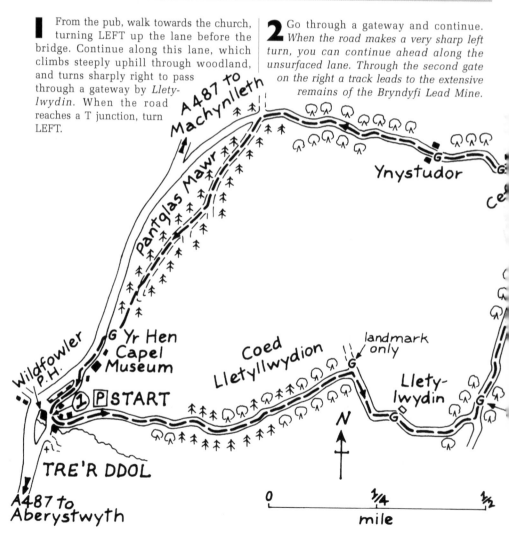

14

After sinking trial levels, work began here in earnest in 1881. The mine was designed by D C Davies & Son, and initially employed 100 men. Extensive developments at the surface have left well executed buddle circles (a buddle separated the crushed ore from gangue, or ore matrix), wheelpits, ore bins and a crusher house in a remarkably good state of repair. Deposits of ore, however, did not live up to initial expectations, and the mine closed after only a couple of years,

having brought just 24 tons of lead ore to the surface. A tramway connected these workings with others about half-a-mile to the north-east.

3 Follow the lane sharply to the left, and begin gradually to descend. Pass through three gates at *Cefn gweirog*, and another at *Ynystudor*, and continue until the road enters forestry and starts to descend, and a track crosses. Turn LEFT here and walk along the forest road. Ignore tracks off to the left and continue ahead. Gradually the forest road becomes less distinct – look out for a clear woodland path on the right, and maintain your direction along this. It descends to a gate. Go through and turn LEFT to return to the Wildfowler pub.

Yr Hen Capel, in Tre'r ddol, is worth a look. Once a museum which depicted 19thC religious life in Wales, it was housed in this splendid former Wesleyan chapel linked with the origins of the 1859 religious revival, which had such a momentous effect on the social life of rural, and industrial, Wales.

③ gweirog

Bryndyfi Mine

Yr Hen Capel, Tre'r ddol

WALK 8
THE ESTUARY AT YNYS-HIR

DESCRIPTION An easy 4-mile walk around the RSPB (Royal Society for the Protection of Birds) Reserve at Ynys-hir. Initially amidst woods, the walk soon extends into the saltmarsh of the estuary, with excellent views up and down river. There is, of course, excellent bird-life. If you are already an RSPB member, access is free. If you are not, there is an entrance charge, which represents excellent value, and the walk is worth doing at any time of year. Allow 2½ hours.

START From the car park at Ynys-hir RSPB Reserve. There are toilets, and drinks and light snacks are available from a machine. SN 682964.

DIRECTIONS From the Clock Tower in Machynlleth, take the A487 south towards Aberystwyth. After about 6 miles, at Eglwys fach, turn right and follow the signs to the RSPB Reserve and park below the Visitor Centre (09.00-17.00 summer, 10.00-16.00 winter). The reserve is open dawn to dusk all year except Christmas Day. Dogs, except registered assistance dogs, are not allowed on the reserve.

Ynys-hir was purchased by the RSPB in 1969, and has subsequently been enlarged to cover 1056 acres. It is a site of great importance, encompassing several Sites of Special Scientific Interest (SSSI). The cho-

sen route of this walk encompasses many of the habitats available here. The initial part, to the north of the railway line, takes in salt-marsh, peatland and the freshwater pools and ditches by Marian Mawr, a rush dominated field. Returning to the south-west of the RSPB Centre the walk continues through mixed woodlands, parts of which date from the 17thC and were cut for use as charcoal in the lead and iron smelting industries. You then walk through beautiful mixed woodland before crossing marshland on a boardwalk to reach the R S Thomas hide. Your return passes the Ynys-hir hide, with the option of a worthwhile diversion, if you have the time, out to the Breakwater hide.

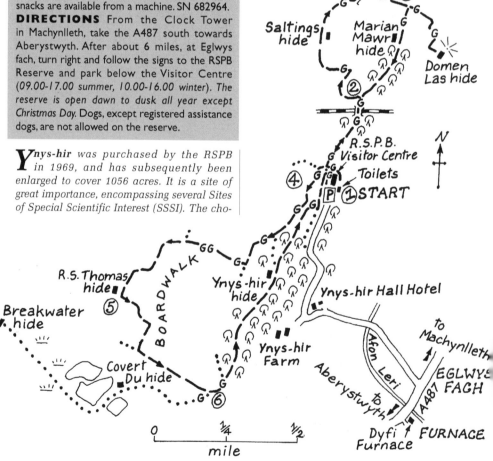

16

Freshwater pools and ditches have been created at Ynys Edwin, Covert Du, Covert Coch and West Marsh, and livestock grazing maintains the saltings for wildfowl in winter. Much of the oak-wood is now fenced to allow seedlings to regenerate, and many indigenous woodland plants have been replanted.

The most important of the habitats at Ynys-hir are the saltmarshes, where important populations of as many as 3000 wigeon, and a modest 100 or so Greenland white-fronted geese may be seen in winter. There are also mallard, teal, shelduck, pintail, red-breasted merganser and goldeneye. Curlews are present throughout the year. Many characteristic woodland species are found in the oakwoods, along with lesser spotted woodpeckers and nuthatches. A few reed warblers may be seen in Covert Du, and there is a heronry in the wood by Domen Las. The characteristic local birds of prey: red kites, hen harriers, merlins and peregrines can be seen all year. Come in May to see carpets of bluebells and wood anemones, or later to enjoy foxgloves and flowering cow-wheat.

It has hosted the BBC's 'Springwatch' programme for several years, and nesting Ospreys at the nearby Cors Dyfi Reserve (along the road towards Machynlleth) are an added spring and summer attraction.

1 Turn LEFT out of the front of reception, and LEFT again to go through a small gate to turn RIGHT onto a track. Go through a gate and continue AHEAD to another gate and go through. Continue AHEAD, passing a seat on the left, to reach a gate. Go through, cross the bridge over the railway and go through another gateway.

2 Turn LEFT on a path signposted towards Saltings hide. Soon the path veers to the right and continues with water on the left and trees to the right. You reach a wooden gate on the left. Go through then veer RIGHT, passing a gate on the left. Pass the Saltings hbide and continue to a gate on the LEFT. Go through this, cross the bridge, turn RIGHT and continue.

3 You reach a signposted path junction. If you wish to visit the Domen Las hide (an

out-and-back diversion) go AHEAD through a gate and then veer left on a clear path. Look out for a small gate on the LEFT into trees, and go through. Continue, soon walking beside a high fence to reach the hide. The views from this hide are particularly good. Now return to the path junction. From the junction take the narrow path which leads uphill towards the Marian Mawr hide, soon going through a gate. Go through the gate and continue, passing a very sturdy 'three-seater-bench' in front of the Marian Mawr hide. Continue along the path to reach the railway bridge crossed on your way out. Cross the bridge, go through a gate and continue AHEAD to the next gate.

4 Go through this and turn RIGHT, crossing a track to reach a gate into woods. Go through and continue on a narrow path through beautiful woodland, eventually reach a gate. Go through and veer LEFT to eventually reach another gate, which you go through. After about 20 yards turn RIGHT through a gate onto a boardwalk. Continue along this, passing through gates. At a boardwalk junction keep AHEAD to eventually veer left to reach the R S Thomas hide, which is up to the right.

5 Turn LEFT here by the snake sculpture and continue along the boardwalk, which twists and turns, passing a large metal dragonfly sculpture, to eventually reach a track, where you turn LEFT and continue.

6 When you reach a junction you can, if you wish, turn right for an out-and-back visit to the Covert Du and Breakwater hides. Otherwise turn LEFT through a gate and continue for a short way to reach a small gate on the RIGHT, signposted to Ynys-hir hide. Go through and continue on a narrow path which climbs through the woods. You pass the Ynys-hir hide on the left just before the path splits. Go to the RIGHT on a narrow path which zig-zags uphill. Follow the path to eventually join a track at a gate. Go through and turn LEFT, continuing along the track and looking out for a small arched gateway on the RIGHT. Go through this to return to the RSPB Visitor Centre.

1 From the Black Lion, walk in the Aberystwyth direction on the lane. Turn sharp LEFT uphill along a footpath (signpost obscure) by *Brynderwen*. The path zig-zags uphill through woods, passes through a gate and continues, to join a track. Turn RIGHT and walk for a short distance to a path which climbs sharp LEFT up the hillside (if you reach the signposts on the main track, you have passed it!).

2 When the path joins a narrow road, continue ahead. When the road bends to the left through a gate, continue AHEAD along the green track (the two apparent routes become one just over the brow).

3 You come to a fence with a stile. Cross this and continue, veering slightly left downhill to a gate. Go through the gate and then veer slightly left downhill. *The original course of the bridleway can be discerned in many places along here, with shallow cuttings through rock being the most obvious clue. Follow this old trackway as closely as you can.* Go through another gate and continue, veering slightly left away from the trees to reach a gate by a small rock outcrop. Go through and zig-zag downhill to join a track by the river. Turn LEFT.

4 Go through a gate and continue on ahead. *This is Cwm Llyfnant, a very pretty valley, with tall rocky cliffs to the left, and the tumbling Llyfnant to the right, all enclosed by trees. It has been designated as an SSSI, and most of the 195 acre site is owned by the RSPB. The middle section has the remnants of ancient woodland, with cliffs and scree on the south* side containing huge boulders rich with ferns and mosses, thriving in the humid oceanic conditions found here. Woods of sessile oak and mountain ash rise from a shrub layer of hazel. Amongst the flora is a sub-species of wood stitchwort in its

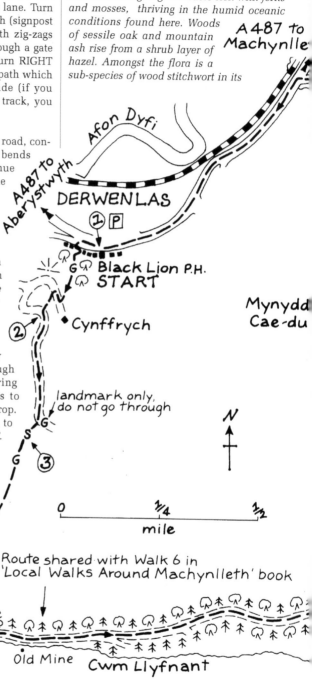

A487 to Machynlleth

Afon Dyfi

A487 to Aberystwyth

DERWENLAS

① P

G Black Lion P.H.

G START

• Cynffrych

②

Mynydd Cae-du

landmark only, do not go through

G
S

N

G ③

0   ¼   ½
mile

G
G
G

Route shared with Walk 6 in 'Local Walks Around Machynlleth' book

Old Mine

④ Old Mine   Cwm Llyfnant

18

only known location in Ceredigion. A small cave close to the summit contains luminous moss, and the summit is rich with bilberry and broad buckler-fern. At the level of the river there is an old tunnel entrance to the left, and another very short tunnel a little further along on the right. These were exploratory mine workings only, with no evidence of production. Stay on the main track, ignoring branches off to the right. You gradually climb away from the river.

5 You leave the woods through a gate. Turn LEFT to follow a rough track, with a stone wall on your right. Cross a gate and continue. Go through the next gate and walk downhill to join the road.

6 Now walk ahead along this quiet road until it joins the main road. Turn LEFT to return to the start at Derwenlas.

Mynydd Garth Gwynion

Coed Garth Gwynion

Garth-Owen

Nant Rhisglog

Derwenlas ('green oak') used to be, as the highest navigable point on the river, the port for Machynlleth. Indeed one of the riverside fields was called 'Cae Wharf', the field of the wharf, and there were three quays: Tafan Isa, Quay Ellis and Quay Ward. 40,000 ft of timber, 15,000 oak poles, 500 tons of bark, 1500 tons of slate and 586 tons of lead were exported in 1847. It was served by 'flats' and sloops, and shipbuilding

WALK 9
DERWENLAS & CWM LLYFNANT

DESCRIPTION A 4½ mile walk where superb views over the Dyfi Valley are soon replaced by the intimacy of the beautiful Cwm Llyfnant, a remote and beautiful valley where the main road traffic seems miles away! The return is along a quiet minor road beside the Nant Rhisglog. Allow 3 hours.

START From the Black Lion pub at Derwenlas. SN 721991.

DIRECTIONS From the Clock Tower in Machynlleth, take the A487 south towards Aberystwyth. The first village on this road is Derwenlas, 2 miles from the town. Park on the left, by the Black Lion.

was carried on here until 1869 when the last craft, the 'Rebecca', was launched. The wharves were isolated when the course of the Dyfi was diverted away from the village when the railway track was laid, and they soon silted up, although the wharf downstream at Morben continued trading for a while. Indeed it was the building of the railway which brought the last glorious flush of trade to the river. Derwenlas was also served by the Corris Tramway (currently undergoing restoration at the Corris end), which was originally worked by gravity above Machynlleth, and horse drawn below. Later, steam locomotives were used. There were, at one time, plans for the railway junction now sited downstream at Dovey Junction to be positioned here: it would have been less exposed to storm and flood; the bridge over the Dyfi would have been cheaper to build; and it would have given a rail connection to Pennal, on the northern side.

The Black Lion pub at Derwenlas, a handsome and cosy place some 450 years old, at one time stood beside the old Machynlleth to Aberystwyth turnpike road, and also served the quays.

19

WALK 10

SALMON, SEWIN & THE DYFI BRIDGE

DESCRIPTION It takes no time at all to enter open country down by the Dyfi, and soon you will be enjoying a stroll beside one of Wales' best salmon and sewin (wild sea trout) rivers. When the fish are 'running' in the late summer and autumn you may well see them forging a way upstream to their spawning grounds. Salmon are still caught under licence by hand drawn net near the estuary – indeed it is one of the last rivers in Wales where wild fish can be taken and sold on. From Pont ar Ddyfi you return across the flood plain, with fine views up and down the valley. An easy 1¾ miles, so allow about an hour.
START From the Clock Tower, Machynlleth. SH 745008.

I From the Clock Tower walk towards the station and take the first LEFT by Royal House, to walk down the Garsiwn. *Royal House recently underwent extensive renovation. It is believed to be the oldest surviving building in Machynlleth, although the front was altered in the 19th-century to accommodate a shop. David Gam, who attempted to assassinate Owain Glyndŵr, was imprisoned here between 1404-12, and tradition has it that Charles I stayed here in 1643. An ancient well has been discovered. Garsiwn translates as 'Garrison', and recalls a time when soldiers assembled here around 1570 before going to Ireland. The Garsiwn Well would have constituted an important water supply for the men and their horses. The Corris Tramway, which connected the Corris Steam Railway with the port of Derwenlas, once ran across Garsiwn Square. It was first used in 1859, the carriages being horse drawn.* Turn RIGHT at the bottom then veer left to walk between houses in the far left-hand corner of a 'triangle'. Walk down a narrow path between houses (ignore the field gate on the left) to go through a metal kissing-gate and enter a field. Now walk with the fence

to your left, cross a stile and continue with a ditch to your left to reach a rough bridge and a stile. Cross these and continue to another stile ahead – *and don't forget to turn around for an unusual view of the Machynlleth skyline*. It can be quite muddy here during wet weather. Cross this and maintain your direction towards the railway and a prominent crossing sign.

2 Cross a stile and climb up to the line, then STOP, LOOK AND LISTEN. Only when you are certain it is safe to to so, cross the line and walk down to the stile opposite, and cross this. Follow the path through a patch of rough ground and cross a stile to join a track. Now cross a ladder stile opposite to walk on a concessionary path between field boundaries on Tir Gofal land, where access with a dog may be restricted during lambing time. When you reach an open field veer LEFT to reach another ladder stile. Cross this and carry on ahead to reach the Afon Dyfi.

3 Turn RIGHT and walk with the river to your left. Cross a stile and continue to eventually reach another stile, which you cross. Carry on to reach a stile beside Pont ar Ddyfi. Cross this and turn RIGHT to walk along the dedicated roadside track towards Machynlleth. There are good views up and down the Dyfi Valley, and you will also see the interesting buildings of the Dyfi Eco Park. When the track ends just before the railway bridge and station carefully cross the road and negotiate your way to the raised pavement under the bridge. Continue back towards the Clock Tower, passing the War Memorial and Y Tabernacl on your left. *Y Tabernacl opened in 1986 as a centre for the performing arts, the Tabernacl hosts concerts throughout the year, and a renowned festival in late August. The beautiful auditorium holds 400 people seated on pitch pine pews, where they, and the performers, revel in the buiilding's perfect acoustics. The Museum of Modern Art Wales has six elegant exhibition spaces, hosting the Tabernacl Collection of Modern Welsh Art and a series of temporary exhibitions. There are workshops, and an annual art competition.*

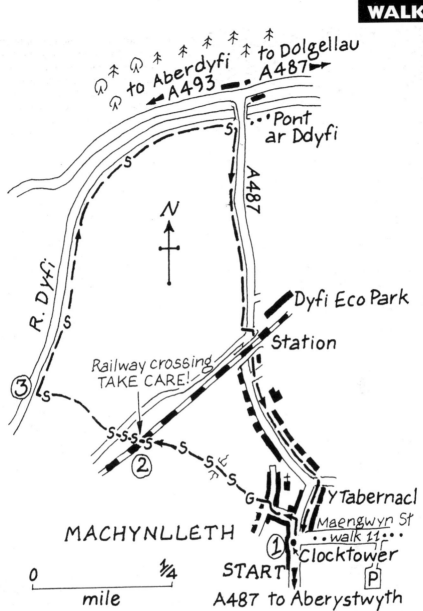

to Aberdyfi to Dolgellau
A493 — · A487 ►

···Pont
ar Ddyfi

A487

N

R. Dyfi

Dyfi Eco Park

Station

Railway crossing
TAKE CARE!

③

②

Ⓖ

Y Tabernacl

Maengwyn St
··walk 11···

MACHYNLLETH

①
START

Clocktower

P

0   ¼

mile

A487 to Aberystwyth

About the author, David Perrott . . .

Having moved with his wife Morag to Machynlleth from London over thirty years ago, his love of this area remains as strong now as it was then. The founder of Kittiwake publishing, he enjoys walking and cycling around Machynlleth which, lying on the southern border of The Snowdonia National Park and in the Dyfi Valley, still remains friendly, unspoilt and relatively undiscovered. He is the author of the National Trail Guide to Glyndŵr's Way.

WALK 11
FORGE & THE GOLF COURSE

DESCRIPTION As with all of the walks which start in Machynlleth, in no time at all you are away from the built-up area and walking through glorious countryside, this time initially beside the Afon Dulas and then on the road to the tiny village of Forge. You gain height along a fine green track and soon you are walking over the golf course on your return to the town. It is then an easy climb to the summit at Parc Common for a final view over the town before you return. An easy 3-mile walk, which will take about 1½ hours.

START From the Clock Tower, Machynlleth. SH 745008.

1 From the Clock Tower walk along Maengwyn Street, continuing ahead when the road forks to the right opposite a fish & chip shop. Pass the access road to the golf club, pass an electricity sub-station and then turn RIGHT down steps at a break in the crash barrier, before the road crosses the river. Veer left to walk beside the river and when you reach a ladder stile, cross it and continue beside the river. When you reach another stile, cross it and continue. You then approach farm buildings, where you turn right to walk beside them, then turn LEFT to go through a gate. Turn RIGHT to walk up to a road.

2 Turn LEFT, cross the road when it is safe to do so, and continue. When you reach a road junction by the bridge in Forge, continue AHEAD for a few paces to reach a gate on the right. *There was a bronze age mine in Forge called Ogof Widdon, the Witches Cave. There were also five fulling mills, or pandys, taking their power from the Afon Dulas, but the last closed in 1937. Electricity used to be generated at Dolgau Farm – with the system being set up in 1931.* Go through and turn half-LEFT to walk uphill on a fine green track, which soon veers right, then left, and continues to climb to reach a gate at the top of the field.

3 Go through the gate and turn RIGHT to walk along a lane. When you reach two gates ahead, go through the LEFT-hand one, leaving the road and following a track with a fence to the right and, soon, a great view ahead. As the vista opens, swing LEFT along a faint track (leaving your earlier track beneath you to the right) to walk towards a gully, with rocks on either side. Walk through the gully, emerging on a narrow path which curves right to overlook the golf course. Now walk across the course, TAKING GREAT CARE to avoid golf balls and keeping off the 'greens', heading towards the right-hand side of a bracken-covered hill ahead, and some black-and-white posts by the road.

4 When you reach the road, turn LEFT and walk along the road to a cattle grid, where you turn RIGHT and then veer RIGHT uphill along a path. Follow this path over the hill and down to a gate, passing the gorsedd stones erected for the 1938 eisteddfod. Go through the gate and turn LEFT to return to the start, first passing the Old Court House on the left – *an inscription on the building reads '1628 Owen Pugh io uxor', with the date marking the rebuilding of an earlier structure. 'Uxor' is Latin and means wife, but apparently there is no established translation for 'io'. This was once the court house for the Lordship of Cyfeiliog* – and the Old Parliament House on the right – *2004 was the six-hundred-years anniversary of the crowning of Owain Glyndŵr as Prince of Wales in Machynlleth, and it was near here that he held a parliament. Although having been rebuilt, the building on the left is a fine example of a late medieval Welsh town house, one of only eight Grade I listed buildings in Montgomeryshire. It contains a Glyndŵr exhibition. The Institute, on the right, was built in 1911, although it appears to be much older. The toll stones which once stood in Pentrerhedyn Street and Doll Street are kept upstairs.*

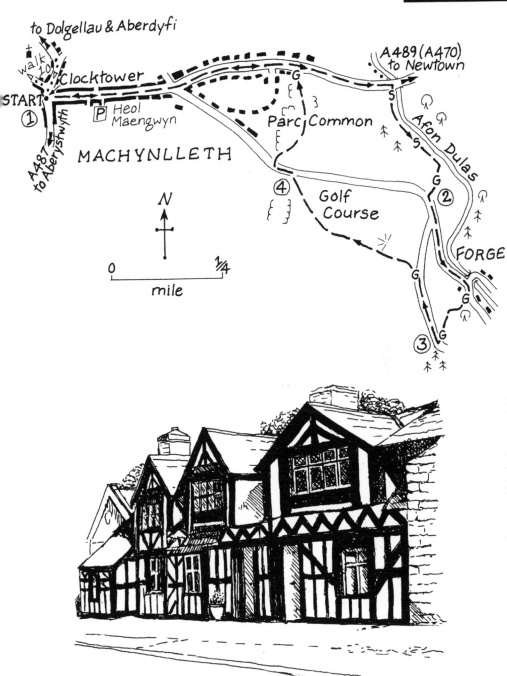

The Old Court House

WALK 12
CAT & MYNYDD LLWYN-GWERN

DESCRIPTION On the initial part of this walk you will enjoy an energetic climb, passing the Centre for Alternative Technology to reach an area of forest. The views from the top over the Dulas Valley are excellent. It is then an easy downhill walk to the southern end of Esgairgeiliog (where there is a little local pub), with the return along a quiet lane.

Please note that while you may walk up the right of way beside the entrance to the CAT, if you wish to visit the site (and we strongly recommend that you do), you MUST pay and secure a ticket. If you live in the SY20 postal area, bring evidence of your address along and you can get a FREE pass! This is a moderate 3 mile walk, so allow about 2 hours.

START From the Clock Tower in Machynlleth follow signs for Dolgellau, on the A487. The Centre for Alternative Technology is signed off to the right after about 3 miles. (SH 753044).

I From the entrance to the Centre for Alternative Technology car park, to the LEFT of the cliff railway station and the access road, follow the signposted 'Woodland Walk' uphill. *The late Gerard Morgan-Grenville, the Centre for Alternative Technology's founding spirit, recalled clearly 'the autumn day in 1973 when I threaded my way up through thick rhododendrons to the level area where CAT, as it is affectionately known, now stands. The golden leaves were falling slowly in the still air and the sense of timelessness, which I have always associated with this place, struck me forcibly. In such seclusion, I had the feeling that something new, some fresh and saner way of living, might be demonstrated'. From this vision CAT came into existence, presenting practical solutions to our current problems of over-consumption and degredation of the environment.*

But it was all a bit strange at first: '...we didn't know what on earth they wanted here. It was an old quarry, which had been closed

for years' said one local resident... 'but they have turned full circle and now make contemporary those methods of generating power which were used in the Dyfi valley in the 40s and 50s' said another. Now fresh organic fruit, flowers and vegetables grow where slate was once quarried, energy conservation is demonstrated and clean energy generation contributes power to the site. There is a fine bookshop, a café serving vegetarian food and a children's playground. When you reach the top of this path turn LEFT up steps signed to 'Wind Turbines'. When you reach the top of this path, cross the stile on the left and then walk half-RIGHT uphill to a gate, with a wind turbine over to your left.

2 Go through the gate, turn RIGHT, and then after a few paces veer LEFT to follow a faint grassy track uphill. When the track is no longer visible maintain your direction up the initial slope until you reach a more pronounced low hill. Veer slightly LEFT to walk around the side of this until you see a gate and stile into the forestry ahead, beside a tall wind turbine. Go over the stile and follow the track until you join a forest road at a T junction, where you turn LEFT. Follow the track for a little over 100 metres, then turn LEFT down a clear forest track.

3 Cross the waymarked stile and walk in the direction indicated by the waymark, roughly parallel to a stream on the left. As you approach a cwm, head towards a waymarked gate. Go through the gate, pass a small pond on the right and follow the distinct track, which zig-zags and continues around the slope. Go through a gate and bear LEFT downhill along a fine green lane beside a fence. Go through a gate and continue ahead along the track. Cross a small stream and carry on. Go through a gate with a splendid 'Beware of the Bull' sign on the other side (don't worry – we are told it has been many years since a bull was kept here!) and carry on.

4 Cross a stile beside a gate by some houses and veer right down to the road. Turn LEFT along the minor road to return to the Centre for Alternative Technology.

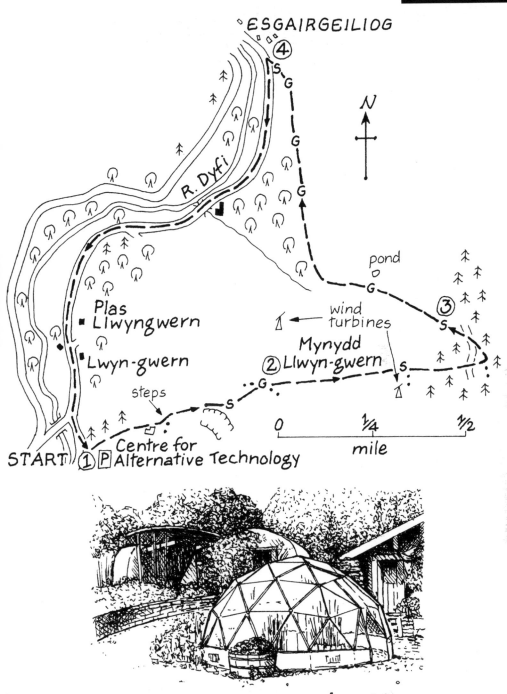

ESGAIRGEILIOG

④

N

R. Dyfi

pond

③

Plas
Llwyngwern

wind
turbines

Lwyn-gwern

Mynydd
②Llwyn-gwern

steps

0   ¼   ½
        mile

START ① P Centre for
          Alternative Technology

The Centre for Alternative Technology gardens

WALK 13

THE THREE PEAKS VIEW

DESCRIPTION A fine 4½ mile walk in the hilly country to the east of Machynlleth. Starting from the church at Darowen, the walk passes a splendid standing stone and a handsomely converted mill before climbing to the summit of Fron Goch, a modest enough hill but one with exceptional views. Allow 3 hours.

START From the parking area opposite St Tudur's church, Darowen. SH 830018.

DIRECTIONS From the Clock Tower in Machynlleth, take the A489 east towards Newtown. After passing through Penegoes, take the next turning on the right, signposted to Darowen. Pass through Abercegir, then fork left steeply uphill to Darowen. Park on the village green, opposite the church.

I From the village green, walk down the lane opposite the church, behind the old school buildings. When the tarmac ends at *Tan-llan* farm, continue down the lane, which can get very wet after rain. Cross the first stream and continue to the second, which is crossed by footbridge. The track climbs to reach a cross-tracks, at the entrance to *Pwlliwrch* farm. Continue straight ahead. *Just before the track starts to drop down towards Tal-y-Wern, before a lane leaves to the left, look over the gate on the right to see the standing stone 'Maen llwyd'. This stone is one of three which were thought to mark a 'noddfa', or sanctuary. Those suspected of wrong-doing were given a head start to reach the area enclosed by the stones and, if successful, were allowed to go free. The stone here, the largest of the two surviving, stands in a field known as Cae yr hen eglwys (old church field). A ley-line through the surviving stones links these with the church. The third stone, Carreg y Noddfa, once stood to the east of Cwm Bychan Mawr, but was broken for building stone around 1860. There is no right of way into the field.*

2 When you come to a T junction at the entrance to *Rhosdyrnog*, turn RIGHT

and walk down to the road, where you turn LEFT. At the village of Tal-y-Wern, turn RIGHT downhill, following the sign for Melinbyrhedyn. The road climbs steeply, and twists and turns. Soon you reach a track on your right, marked by a *Llwybr Cyhoeddus* sign. Turn RIGHT through the gate and follow the track, which enters trees and soon accompanies a stream to the right. Walk through trees to emerge at a field opposite a handsome converted mill. Walk diagonally LEFT up the field to a converted farmhouse.

3 Climb the gate below the house, and walk down the lane at the front of the house. Go through the gate at the bottom of the lane, and turn LEFT to walk along the road.

4 Shortly before the road bends away to the right, take the way-marked grassy track half-RIGHT uphill. Continue, crossing the road and maintaining your direction uphill. Go through a gate and then immediately leave the track to walk half-RIGHT up the field, to a gate in a field corner. Go through the gate and turn LEFT. Walk to a gateway on the left, go through and turn RIGHT, to walk with a fence on your right.

5 You reach a gate. Go through and walk to a stile to the right. Cross the stile and immediately turn RIGHT to walk steeply uphill, with a fence on your right. Continue until you reach a gate on your right. DO NOT go through the gate, but walk to the LEFT up the green track opposite. When you reach another gate, DO NOT go through, but turn RIGHT to walk uphill. Continue to the top of Fron Goch. *The summit here is a mere 930 ft high, enclosed by the faint remains of the ditch and wall of a Romano-British hill fort, yet it offers stunning views. On a clear day you will see the sea at Aberdyfi, and the summits of Cadair Idris, Aran Fawddwy and Pumlumon Fawr.* Walk downhill, with the village of Darowen ahead to the right.

Bryn llwyn

Cattle gric

To Abercegir & Machynlle

6 Cross the stile beside a gate, turn sharply LEFT and walk downhill towards a gate. Do not go through but turn RIGHT to rejoin the right of way. Walk with a hedge on your left. Go through a gate and follow the track to another gate. Go through and walk

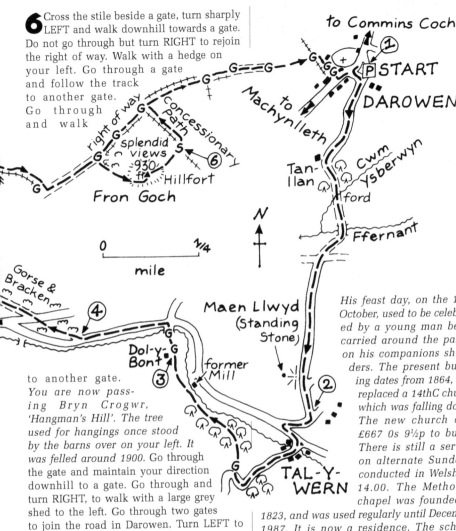

to another gate. You are now passing Bryn Crogwr, 'Hangman's Hill'. The tree used for hangings once stood by the barns over on your left. It was felled around 1900. Go through the gate and maintain your direction downhill to a gate. Go through and turn RIGHT, to walk with a large grey shed to the left. Go through two gates to join the road in Darowen. Turn LEFT to return to the start.

Darowen stands at a height of around 600ft, and commands a splendid view over the foothills of the Pumlumon range. The church is built on a raised circular site, giving a clue to its antiquity, and this, combined with the accompanying standing stones, suggests that the village may have been of considerable importance at the time of the Wessex Culture, around 2000 BC. St Tudurs' was founded in the 7thC, and it is claimed that the saint is buried here.

His feast day, on the 15th October, used to be celebrated by a young man being carried around the parish on his companions shoulders. The present building dates from 1864, and replaced a 14thC church which was falling down. The new church cost £667 0s 9½p to build. There is still a service on alternate Sundays, conducted in Welsh, at 14.00. The Methodist chapel was founded in 1823, and was used regularly until December 1987. It is now a residence. The school, now also a residence, was opened in 1841, and extended in 1871. It finally closed in 1971. The 18thC saw the heyday of the village, when lead was mined locally at Cwm Bychan, and the community had a blacksmith, two shops and two pubs. The origins of the name Darowen suggests that it may mean 'Owain's Oaks', referring to the time when Owain Glyndŵr's army was camped in the area, but this explanation lacks any true antiquity. Some suggest Owain may have died not far from here.

27

WALK 14
THE DAROWEN PANORAMA

DESCRIPTION This moderate 3-mile walk offers views of the mid-Wales summits that are every bit as exciting as those found on the 'Dolgellau panoramas'. Initially you climb quite gently though fields as the summits of Cadair Idris and Aran Fawddwy, along with their associated ranges, gradually open up to your left. Turn around and there is Pumlumon peaking over the ridge beyond Carn Hyddgen. Mynydd y Cemmaes frames the north-east, with the Tarrens stretching away towards the sea in the north-west. This circuit has been made possible by the recent efforts of the Powys footpath team – as a consequence one short section is still 'bedding in' with use. But route finding is easy, so there should be no problems. Allow 2 hours for the walk, plus more time to savour the views. See **Walk 13** for details of Darowen.

START From the parking area opposite St Tudur's church, Darowen. SH 830018.

DIRECTIONS From the Clock Tower in Machynlleth, take the A489 east towards Newtown. After passing through Penegoes, take the next turning on the right, signposted to Darowen. Pass through Abercegir, then fork left steeply uphill to Darowen. Park on the village green, opposite the church.

1 Facing the church, turn RIGHT. Ignore the road which goes downhill behind the parking area, but turn right almost immediately by Llys Tudor to walk gently uphill along a lane. After about 200 yards climb steps up to a stile on the LEFT. Cross this and walk half-RIGHT across the field, climbing easily to a gate to the left of a small covered reservoir. Go through and, keeping the fence on your left, walk to the next gate. Go though and carry on, still beside the fence, to the next gate. Go through and carry on straight ahead uphill to a stile to the right of a gate.

2 Cross the stile and walk half-RIGHT uphill to a small wooden gate in the corner of the field. *To your left there is a panorama stretching from the Tarrens to Cadair Idris and on to Aran Fawddwy.* Go through the gate and continue, now with a fence on the right, to a stile, which you cross, and on to gate. Go through, staying beside the fence and passing an area of rushes, where the ground can be quite wet. The fence bends to left to reach a stile.

3 Cross the stile into woodland and immediately turn LEFT to walk on a rough path beside the fence, where you start to descend. Cross a tiny stream and continue, following waymark posts which direct you downhill through a felled plantation, now re-growing as a species-rich environment. Soon you will emerge at a forest track opposite a small green waymark post.

4 Turn RIGHT to walk along the track. *To your left is Mynydd y Cemmaes.* Continue until you reach a track on the right, just before the track you are on bends quite sharply right. Turn RIGHT here to walk steeply uphill, ignoring any overgrown tracks off to the left or right. Carry on uphill, and eventually the track becomes grassy and you reach a gate. Go through and continue with a fence on your left until you reach a gate on the LEFT.

5 Go through the gate and turn initially half-RIGHT to walk around two hawthorn trees, then veer RIGHT to skirt a low hill on the right. Soon the roof of a barn ahead come into view. Veer to the right of this looking for a small gate. GO through and continue AHEAD to walk down to the left of Bryn Einon, where you turn RIGHT to follow a track by the house. Continue past the small pond down to the road, where you turn RIGHT along the lane to return to Darowen. *There are splendid views of the Pumlumon range over to your left.*

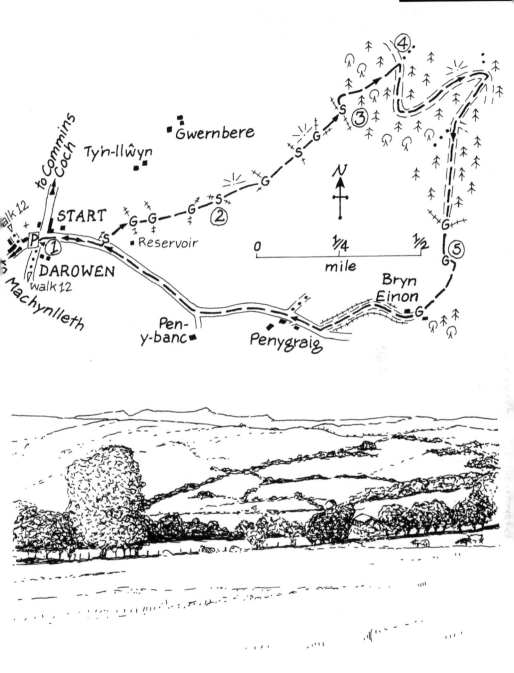

Looking towards Cadair Idris from the Darowen Panorama

WALK 15
A TASTE OF GLYNDŴR

DESCRIPTION Splendid views of the Dyfi Valley feature strongly on this 5 mile walk which, for a good part of the route, shares its course with Glyndŵr's Way. All the paths are clear and wide, although one short stretch can be muddy. Allow 3 hours.
START From Commins Coch. SH 035846.
DIRECTIONS From the Clock Tower in Machynlleth, take the A489 east towards Newtown. At the roundabout at Glantwymyn, take the A470 straight ahead. At Commins Coch, immediately after the road crosses the bridge over the river, turn sharp left to go under the railway. About ¼ mile up the lane, park in the lay-by opposite a grey corrugated iron shed.

1 From the lay-by, continue along the lane, forking LEFT along the signed bridle-path (also to Glyntwymyn). Continue along the track, passing through two gates.

2 Go through a small gate off the track, to walk along the top

and soon the wind-farm on Mynydd y Cemmaes *(Walk 19) comes into view.* Go through this gate and, maintaining your direction,

edge of a field, avoiding the house. Rejoin the track through a second gate, then pass through two more gates to continue along the track. Pass through the next gate and continue, ignoring a track which forks off to the right. Carry on downhill.

3 When the track joins a signed bridleway, turn RIGHT. *You are now on Glyndwr's Way (see below).* When a signed green track branches off to the LEFT, follow this. At a track crossing, continue ahead, up to a gate. Go through, then walk ahead, uphill, to another gate. *There are good views from here,*

30

reach another gate, tucked into the field corner.

4 Go through this gate, and continue downhill along a track to another gate. Go through, cross a tiny stream and follow the track to the left of a farmhouse. Go through the next gate and, as you leave the farm, turn right through a signed gate. The track turns to the right and continues, passing through six gates, curving first left and then right. *There are superb and expansive views from this section over the Dyfi Valley.* Eventually you reach a lane, close to *Gwalia.*

5 Maintain your direction along the lane until it turns sharply right, with a track to the left.

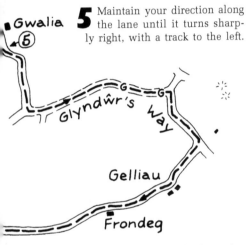

Turn LEFT, going gently uphill along this often muddy track. Pass through two gates to emerge at a road. Turn RIGHT. At the next road junction, turn RIGHT again, leave Glyndwr's Way, and return to the start.

S o who was Glyndŵr? In 1284 Edward I completed England's conquest of Wales, when Llywelyn was killed in a skirmish with English forces at Climery, near Builth Wells. Owain ap Gruffydd (Owain Glyndŵr) was born around 1359, the son of Gryffydd Fychan and descendant of the royal house of Powys. He probably served as an apprentice in law in London, staying at the Inns of Court. Later he became Squire to Henry Bolingbroke, King Richard's cousin, and during this period he would have learned his fighting skills, which he probably honed during campaigns in Scotland and Europe.

In 1398, his military career over, he settled near Sycharth in a moated wooden house, married to Margaret Hanmer and with a 'nest of children'.

In 1400 there was discontent in Wales and Scotland and, on 16 September, Owain was proclaimed Prince of Wales, encouraged by Welsh hatred for the English King and his Marcher Lords. On the 18th September Owain's motley army rode into Ruthin. By the 24th they had raided other towns and were closing upon Welshpool when they were routed near Shrewsbury. Henry VI's army arrived the next day, and subsequently subdued the rebellion. All the rebels, except Owain, were pardoned, but the Welsh as a whole were badly treated by the English parliament.

Rebellion re-occurred in 1401, with Conwy Castle being burned. Owain raised an army, and Henry responded, strengthening garrisons and reinforcing castles. A comet which appeared in the sky in 1402 was taken as an omen, since its tail was said to point towards Wales. Owain's rebellion grew, defeating the English at Pilleth, near Knighton, at a place called Bryn Glas. Owain then moved south, and also blockaded the castles at Harlech and Caernarfon.

By 1404 Owain had secured Wales, taken Harlech Castle and established a Parliament in Machynlleth. He tried to make an alliance with the French, but this came to nothing, although he tried again, calling a Parliament in Machynlleth and sending the Pennal Letter (See Walk **4**).

Eventually King Henry became ill, and gave Prince Henry a free hand to campaign, successfully, in Wales, turning Owain into a fugitive. In 1407 the rebellion faded through starvation and a lack of funds, and Aberystwyth and Harlech Castles, held by Glyndŵr, were under siege. By 1409 both had fallen. In 1410 it was all over.

Owain Glyndŵr faded from history, and was thought to have died on the 20th September 1415 at Monnington-on-Wye, or, perhaps, on an exposed mountain ridge in Gwynedd – and some say at Pwlliwrch, not far from here.

WALK 16
WYNFORD'S VIEW

DESCRIPTION A 6½ mile walk which climbs steadily from Aberhosan to reach a superb viewpoint from which, on a clear day, you will see the summit of Snowdon. The descent skirts a dramatic cwm (valley), with distant views over Cardigan Bay, then continues through gentler country back to the village. Parts of this route are on an ancient track over bare rock, which can be slippery during or after wet weather. Allow 3½ hours.

START From Aberhosan. Please park your car considerately. SN 810974.

DIRECTIONS From the Clock Tower in Machynlleth, take the A489 east towards Newtown, forking right opposite the 'Top Shop Chippie' towards Dylife. After 4 miles turn right as signposted to Aberhosan. As you enter the village, ignore the right fork by the chapel, and continue ahead. Park considerately at the roadside.

1 From the main street in Aberhosan, continue through the village. The tarmac road changes to a track, and climbs gently. Go through two gates, and continue along the track, still climbing. *Stop for a rest and look back to enjoy an extensive view.* Go through the next gate, and continue with forestry to your left. Go through another gate, and continue. Continue through the next gate to reach the Wynford Vaughan Thomas Memorial.

One of Wales' most eminent journalists and broadcasters, Wynford Vaughan Thomas identified this spot as having one of the finest views in Wales. He passed here several times whilst on his 'radio' trips through Wales on foot and horseback. The memorial was sculptured by Ieuan Rees of Llandybie. It originally depicted the great man's features. He was born in 1908 in Swansea, one of three sons of a musician, and joined the BBC as an outside broadcast assistant in 1937. He became BBC War Correspondent in 1942 and never shied way from danger, making the first live broadcast from an RAF bomber over Berlin. Following the War he covered many momentous events, while finding time to make numerous radio programmes about his beloved Wales, and writing several books.

Sadly missed, his infectious enthusiasm and love for his country lives on in his recordings and books.

2 Leave the memorial through the gate onto the road, and turn RIGHT. Continue along the road for about half a mile to a track signed to 'Nature Reserve, Gwarchodle Natur'. Turn RIGHT onto this track, with Glaslyn ahead. When a track branches to the right by a waymark post, turn RIGHT here to continue the walk. *If you have time, you can continue ahead for about one-third of a mile to visit Glaslyn and the Nature Reserve. You can enjoy a ramble around the lake, but DO NOT enter the ravine, as it is slippery and dangerous.* The track on your circular route passes to the right of the ravine, crossing bare rock which is slippery during or after wet weather, so

ABERHOSAN

to Machynlleth

Nant Blaen-y-Cwm

START

Cefnwyrygrug

Coed Esgairfochnant

Nantyfyda

Esgair-Fochnant

TAKE CARE. *On a clear day, you may be able to see Cardigan Bay from here. To the right is Foel Fadian, at 1850 ft, probably the highest point in Montgomeryshire. The highest point on the route of this walk is 1675 ft.* The track turns sharp LEFT at a waymark post, and descends to a gate and stile, crossing a rocky patch.

3 Cross the stile and continue along the track, which continues its descent to another gate. Go through and carry on ahead. Pass through another gate and continue along the track to *Esgair Fochnant*, where you go through two more gates by the farm. Continue ahead.

*T**he quiet little village of Aberhosan** was at one time famous for its craftsmen, who made ornamental bardic chairs for eisteddfodau, Welsh cultural festivals of music and poetry. These days it comes to life on the third Thursday in August, when it stages its annual show. There are the usual art, cookery, flower arranging and vegetable competitions, sheep dog trials, best kept pets and horse-riding, with some livelier and less tasteful games for the local lads. Aberhosan means 'mouth of the River Rhosan'.*

to Machynlleth

Wynford Vaughan Thomas Memorial

to Dylife

Signpost

0 ¼ mile

N

This section is slippery when wet TAKE CARE!

Foel Fadian 1850ft

Bwlch y Craig

Waymark Post

Waymark Post

Cwm Hafod March

Nant Fadian

Glyndŵr's Way

Afon Dulas

Uwch-y-coed

Glaslyn

4 Go through the gate at *Nantyfyda* and follow the road around a hairpin to the right. Go through another gateway and follow the road around to the left. When the road forks, go the RIGHT, uphill. Now stay on this road, passing through two gates at *Cefnwyrygrug*, to return to Aberhosan.

33

WALK 17

WATERFALLS OVER PENNANT

DESCRIPTION A steep descent and an even steeper climb make this an energetic and exciting 5½ mile walk. The rewards for your efforts are stunning views, fine waterfalls and a friendly pub to relax in when you return. However, because of the strenuous nature of this walk, which involves a short, steep section of descent on the outward route, a stream to cross, and a 650-foot climb within about 600 yards on the return, we could not recommend this walk to those with young children, or those who would not be happy negotiating the steep descent and ascent There are, however, no sheer drops by the path, and those who make the effort will enjoy a quite exceptional walk. Allow 3½ hours.

START From the Star Inn, Dylife, but don't park right by the pub if you are not intending to visit. There is plenty of parking space at Dylife. SN 863941.

DIRECTIONS From the Clock Tower in Machynlleth, take the A489 east towards Newtown, forking right opposite the 'Top Shop Chippie' towards Dylife. At Dylife, turn left to park close to the Star Inn.

1 From the Star Inn, walk back to the main road and turn LEFT. Walk along to the head of the valley. *You get a good view of the Ffrwdd Fawr waterfall from here, and a notice board explains that the River Twymyn used to flow from east to west before the last ice age, when a glacier scoured out a 'U' shaped valley. When the ice melted the river changed course and eroded the valley into the 'V' shape we can see. The water falls almost 200 ft, making this cascade one of Wales' highest.* Continue along the road to just beyond a group of conifers, where a track branches to the LEFT. Go through the gate and follow the track. *There are splendid views to the west.*

2 The track forks at two gates. Go through the LEFT-hand gate, but DO NOT follow the clear track ahead. Walk to the LEFT across the grass, to find the clear path which starts to descend steeply. *TAKE GREAT CARE ON THIS INITIAL STRETCH OF PATH.* The short rocky section is soon passed, and the descent becomes more gentle. Maintain your direction downhill, and the path soon becomes a fine green lane. Go through the gate at *Pennant-uchaf* and continue to *Pennant-isaf*, where you pass through four gates and continue along the lane. Cross the bridge at Pentre Cilcwm and pass the new bungalow on the left.

3 Turn LEFT up the track to *Cilcwm-fawr* but DO NOT enter the yard. Instead, go through a gate on the RIGHT, cross a small enclosure and go through a second, way-marked, gate. Turn LEFT and walk up to a third gate, which you go through, continuing ahead, with a fence on the left. Go through a gate ahead, then walk downhill, with a fence on your left. Cross a small stile and continue, now with the fence to your right, and the Afon Twymyn to your left. Cross a small stream, pass a redundant stile and continue. Go through gate ahead, and carry on along the path beside the Twymyn, going through another gate and negotiating muddy patches.

4 The rough path crosses a stream. This can be a little wide after rainfall, so step carefully on stones to keep your feet dry! Now veer to the RIGHT to a gate. Go through and continue uphill, passing a waymark on a tree to the left. Go through the gate ahead and begin the climb up the very steep path, which zig-zags up the mountainside. *Stop regularly to enjoy the splendid views from this path, and catch your breath.*

5 Eventually you reach a stile. Cross it and continue, with the fence to your right. You soon drop down to a stream. Cross the bridge and go through the gate ahead (ignoring the gate further to the right) and turn LEFT up the track. Go through the next gate and walk towards the right hand side of Capel Seion ahead. Go through the gate beside the chapel and continue along the tarmac lane, to return to the Star Inn, for a well earned pint (or whatever you fancy).

*W*hile you are relaxing in the Star Inn, or returning from your walk, you can reflect upon what changes have been wrought in little over 100 years, for in the mid and late 1800s the population of Dylife, 'the place of floods', numbered around 1000, and the mines were amongst the most productive in Wales. Originally worked by the Romans, the mines reached the peak of their production in 1863, when 2571 tons of lead ore were recovered. Over 250 miners were employed, and Dylife had several pubs, a school, post office, church and chapels. It was the discovery of the Llechwedd Ddu lode which brought about the mines' most productive period, initially under the ownership of Williams & Pughe, who carted the ore 14 hilly miles to the port of Derwenlas (see Walk 9) for transhipment. By this time the mine was large enough to admit horses, pulling small wagons on tracks. Several reservoirs were constructed, one of which powered the Martha Wheel, which with a 63 ft diameter was the largest ever built in Wales. Cobden & Bright (Richard Cobden was an exponent of free trade and campaigned for the abolition of the corn laws) bought the mine in 1858 for £24,000, re-equipping to such an extent that it could claim to be the most modern in the country. Output began falling in 1871, but such was the mines' reputation that the Great Dylife Company took it over in 1873. Today little remains to remind us of this once great enterprise.

Pentre Cilcwm

Cilcwm-fawr

N

Hendre

Afon Twymyn

Pennant-isaf

Pennant-uchaf

VERY STEEP PATH

Llwbr y Ceirw

1325 ft

Cwm Bryn-Moel

Craig y Maes

STEEP & ROCKY

landmark only, go through left-hand gate

0   ¼
mile

START
Star Inn

Capel Seion

DYLIFE

to Machynlleth

Waterfall

to Staylittle

WALK 18
TAFOLWERN CASTLE MOUND

DESCRIPTION An initial steady climb on this 7-mile walk soon offers splendid views over the mountains to the south of Llanbrynmair. A gentle descent passes the old mine workings at Cwmbychan-mawr, before returning along the Twymyn valley. A short section of the route passes through some mountainside gorse, prickly for those wearing shorts! Allow 4 hours.
START From Tafolwern. SH 891027.

DIRECTIONS From the Clock Tower in Machynlleth, take the A489 east towards Newtown. At the roundabout at Cemmaes Road, take the A470 ahead. About 9 miles from Machynlleth, approaching Llanbrynmair, the road bends sharply right over the railway. The turn to Tafolwern is on the right after the bridge. Park considerately in Tafolwern.

1 From Tafolwern walk across the bridge and continue along the lane, passing the mound to your left. The lane climbs to the summit of a small hill, where you turn LEFT, and take the LEFT-hand track between

with the hedge on your right. Cross the stile in the field corner, turn RIGHT to cross a gate, and turn immediately LEFT to continue along the track, still climbing gently.

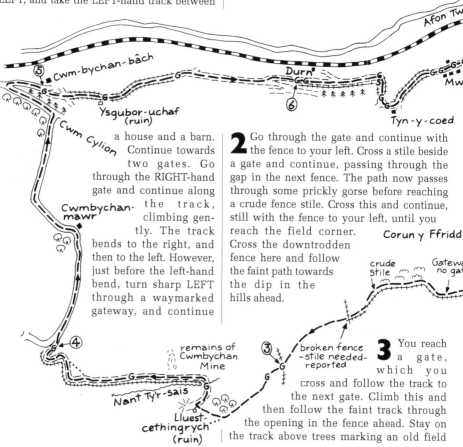

a house and a barn. Continue towards two gates. Go through the RIGHT-hand gate and continue along the track, climbing gently. The track bends to the right, and then to the left. However, just before the left-hand bend, turn sharp LEFT through a waymarked gateway, and continue

2 Go through the gate and continue with the fence to your left. Cross a stile beside a gate and continue, passing through the gap in the next fence. The path now passes through some prickly gorse before reaching a crude fence stile. Cross this and continue, still with the fence to your left, until you reach the field corner. Cross the downtrodden fence here and follow the faint path towards the dip in the hills ahead.

3 You reach a gate, which you cross and follow the track to the next gate. Climb this and then follow the faint track through the opening in the fence ahead. Stay on the track above trees marking an old field

36

boundary. Immediately beyond this, turn half-RIGHT downhill towards a ruin, to join a track. *There are excellent views from here.* Turn RIGHT and walk down to a gate. Go through and turn LEFT. *Up to your right are the remains of Cwmbychan lead mine. This site was probably first worked by the Romans, and was revived during the 19thC. Work ended here in 1875.* Continue along the track, passing through a gate and following it until it joins a road through another gate.

4 Maintain your direction along the road, and following the it past the forestry entrance R22 and on to the track which turns sharp RIGHT up to *Cwm-Bychan-Bach.*

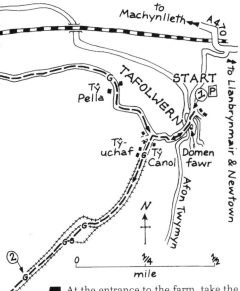

5 At the entrance to the farm, take the RIGHT-hand gate into a field, and walk with the fence on your left. A rough track crosses as you enter an old hollow lane ahead. Continue along this hollow lane, going through a gate beside the ruins of *Ysgubor-uchaf.* The track bends to the left and eventually reaches an old wooden gate. Go through and stay on the track, ignoring a blocked track to your left. The forestry plantation has been cleared here, but just before trees appear again on your left, fork LEFT down a green track (if you reach a major forestry road, you have gone 100yds too far!).

6 Go through two gates above the red brick house by the railway, and continue. Cross a stile beside a gate and follow the lane around to the right. Go through a gate and walk to the left, passing through another gate in front of the black-and-white house *Tyn-y-coed.* Follow the track to *Mwyars,* and continue through four gateways to join the road. Continue along the road. *Just before the road bends to the right at Ty Pella, look to the north across the valley to see Pentremawr. This was built on the site of Cynddelw Brydydd Mawr's house. He was a 12thC warrior-poet, friend of Owen Cyfeiliog (see below) and ranked amongst the best poets Europe.* Go through the gateway at *Ty Pella* and continue along the road back to the start.

T *he mound marks the site of Tafolwern Castle, with the cottage opposite standing in what was the open courtyard, or bailey. Originally known as Walwern, it was the home of Owen Cyfeiliog during the 12thC. A wooden building, it was described by his friend Cynddelw Brydydd Mawr (see above) as 'A'r castell eurog costwych – a costly gilded castle', and stood in the centre of what was at that time a marsh. It was granted to Cyfeiliog by Madoc ap Maredudd, last Prince of a united Powis.*

Cyfeiliog was a poet and one of the Princes of Powis, at a time when Powis occupied roughly what we now know as Montgomeryshire. He was on good terms with Henry II, King of England (1154-89), which did nothing to endear him to his neighbours. One of these, Hywel ab Ieuan, captured Tafolwern in 1161, but Cyfeiliog soon regained control, switching his allegiance to his over-lord Owen Gwynedd, and marrying his daughter. Together they fought against the English invasion in 1165. But the following year Cyfeiliog again switched his allegiance back to the English, and his neighbours invaded his territory in 1171. Cyfeiliog retired to Strata Marcella, and died peacefully there in 1197.

Tafolwern was last mentioned in 1244 when Cyfeiliog's land was invaded by David, Prince of Gwynedd. A request was made to Henry II for fifty knights to defend the castle. The mound is private.

WALK 19
FARMING THE WIND

DESCRIPTION Choose a clear day for this 7-mile walk if you can, when the effort involved in climbing Mynydd y Cemmaes and negotiating the boggy patches will be amply repaid with stunning views along the Dyfi Valley, as far as Aberdyfi and out to sea. You will also get a close look at the Cemmaes Wind Farm. The route is not too difficult to follow, but it is wet and boggy in two or three places. Allow 4 hours.
START By the village hall at Cwm Llinau. SH 847078.
DIRECTIONS From the Clock Tower in Machynlleth, take the A489 east towards Newtown. At the roundabout at Cemmaes Road, turn left onto the A470, and continue through Cemmaes to reach Cwm Llinau. Turn RIGHT here and park considerately on the grass beside the village hall.

I Walk up the lane, after half-a-mile passing the entrance to the caravan park on your left. Carry on along the lane and, where the road forks, go LEFT downhill. Continue, going through a gate. When the track forks, carry on ahead to the next gate. Go through and continue steadily climbing along the now pleasantly grassy track, with a stone wall to your right. *It is worth stopping for a rest, and looking back to enjoy the view.*

2 When the stone wall ends, go through an gate on your RIGHT, and walk diagonally across rough ground towards a waymark post and a stream in a ravine. Continue with the stream tumbling down on your right, negotiating the rough ground and following the waymark posts. As you draw level with trees on your right, you pass another waymark post and continue along-side the stream, which you eventually step across as you reach the corner of the forest. Walk towards the gate.

3 Go through the gate into the forestry plantation, and veer left as waymarked along the clearing. Continue ahead and slightly right as waymarked at the next junction, and reach a gate. Go through, turn RIGHT and walk towards the wind farm, with the fence to your right. The ground is wet and boggy in places here.

4 When you reach a gate, go through and veer LEFT around a summit to meet a track. Turn LEFT. *The view from here towards Aberdyfi and the mountains of Cadair Idris, on a clear day, is quite stunning. It is worth stopping for a while to enjoy it.* Continue along the service track through the wind farm. *The aero-generators look very large when seen from close-up. The blades began spinning late 1992, and the wind farm was officially opened by the Secretary of State for Wales in early 1993. Initially twin bladed generators were installed, but these were later replaced with the more common three-bladed type. Generators to the west of the track were also resited further east, away from the ridge, to avoid extreme turbulence during gales.*

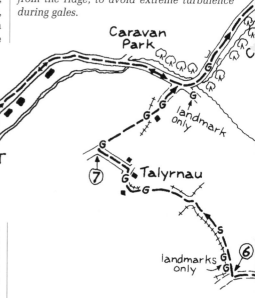

5 Cross a cattle-grid on the track and veer half-RIGHT away from the track over rough grassland, to reach a boggy patch with a fence just beyond the head of a cwm (valley). Pick your way across the wet ground to pick up a good wide track which goes steeply downhill. Go through a gate and continue. *Again the view ahead is splendid.* The track becomes 'green'.

6 You reach another gate. DO NOT go through, but turn RIGHT to walk downhill, with the hedge to your left. Cross a stile and continue to a gate. Go through this and carry on with the hedge now to your right. Go through the next gate and continue, ignoring the first gate to your right. Continue to a gate down to your right, and go through. Walk along the road, and follow it as it turns left.

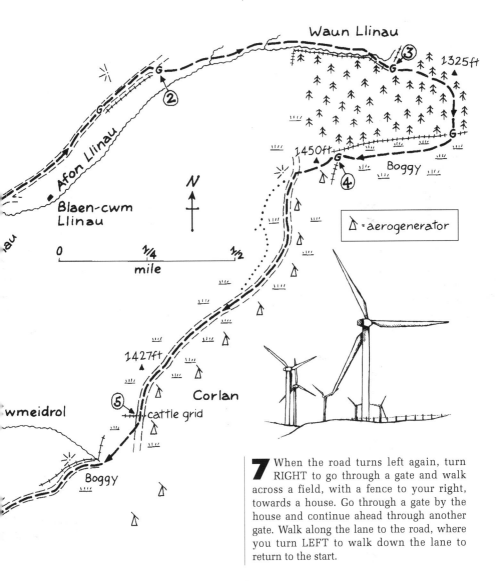

7 When the road turns left again, turn RIGHT to go through a gate and walk across a field, with a fence to your right, towards a house. Go through a gate by the house and continue ahead through another gate. Walk along the lane to the road, where you turn LEFT to walk down the lane to return to the start.

WALK 20
CEMMAES WOODLANDS

DESCRIPTION This strenuous 3-mile walk takes you from the village of Cemmaes over the Afon Dyfi and very steeply up through Coed-Dolfonddu to enjoy a tremendous view of Aran Fawddwy. You return through a remote valley and up a wooded cwm (valley). A short diversion in the village then takes you to the Penrhos Arms and the church. Allow about 2 hours.

START From the parking area at the entrance to Maes-y-llan, on the left as you enter Cemmaes. SH 838060.

DIRECTIONS From the Clock Tower in Machynlleth, take the A489 east towards Newtown. At the roundabout at Cemmaes Road, turn left onto the A470, and continue to Cemmaes.

Leave Maes-y-llan, cross the bridge and turn LEFT onto a footpath beside the stream. Soon cross a footbridge and walk with the water now on your right. Join a road and turn RIGHT to walk by the Afon Dyfi. *Soon you pass the remains of the old railway line between Cemmaes Road to Dinas Mawddwy.* Continue, crossing Pont Rhydygwail, to reach a T-junction, where you turn RIGHT. Continue for 200 yards to reach a gate on the left.

reach an obvious track, where you turn LEFT. Follow this as it veers RIGHT uphill. After about 200 or so yards take the right fork more steeply uphill. At the point where a gate ahead JUST comes into view, turn RIGHT to climb very steeply up through the woods (there isn't a clearly defined path yet) to eventually reach a fence with a gate, which won't be far away. Go through the gate, walk ahead for about 25 yards of so, then turn right, to walk with woodland over to the right. *Soon you will enjoy a wonderful view of Aran Fawddwy.*

3 Go through a wooden field gate in the fence AHEAD and follow the green path half LEFT as it curves downhill. Join a track to the right and continue downhill to pass through two gates between farm buildings. Follow the track to the left to reach a wooden gate. Go through this and and continue with a fence on your left. Pass through a wooden gate and continue, to eventually ford a small stream and reach a gate.

4 Go through the gate and turn very sharp LEFT to follow a rough path uphill beside a cwm. Go through a gate and continue ahead to rejoin your outward route at a gate.

5 As you reach Cemmaes you can take the wooden footbridge on the LEFT, and follow the path beside the Dyfi and then up to the main road opposite the Penrhos Arms – *which was visited by George Borrow in the 1860s.* Turn LEFT to visit St Tydecho's church, or RIGHT to return to your car.

2 Turn LEFT through the gate and walk AHEAD uphill with the remains of an overgrown hedgerow to your right. Enter woods and continue for a short way to

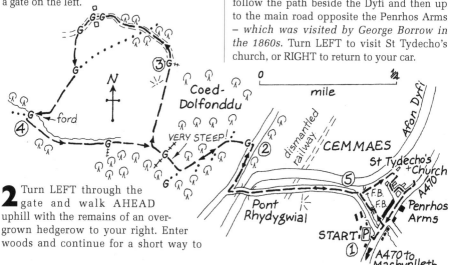